Tasmanian Devil
Nighttime Scavenger

by Joyce L. Markovics

Consultant: Nick Mooney,
Tasmanian Wildlife Biologist

BEARPORT
PUBLISHING

New York, New York

Credits

Cover and Title Page, © Ian Waldie/Getty Images; TOC, © Patsy A. Jacks/Shutterstock; 4, © W.L. Crowther Library, State Library of Tasmania; 5, Courtesy of Nick Mooney; 6, © Klein & Hubert/ Biosphoto/Peter Arnold Inc.; 7, © Courtesy Linnean Society of London; 8, © Rachael Bowes/Alamy; 9, Courtesy of Nick Mooney; 10, © Patsy A. Jacks/Shutterstock; 11, Courtesy of Nick Mooney; 13, © Michael Dick/Animals Animals-Earth Scenes; 13TR, © Wrennie/iStockphoto; 13BL, © Martin Rugner/Superstock; 14, Courtesy of Nick Mooney; 15, © Jeanne White/Photo Researchers, Inc.; 16, © Martin Zwick/Woodfall/Photoshot; 17, Courtesy of Nick Mooney; 18, Courtesy of Nick Mooney; 19, Courtesy of Nick Mooney; 20, Paul A. Souders/Corbis; 21, © Anoek DeGroot/AFP/Getty Images; 22, Courtesy of Nick Mooney; 23, © Dave Watts/NHPA/Photoshot; 24, © Adam Pretty/ Getty Images; 25, Courtesy of Nick Mooney; 26, © Ian Waldie/Getty Images; 27, © Martin Zwick/ Woodfall/Photoshot; 28, © Paul A. Souders/Corbis; 29T, © Dave Watts/Alamy; 29B, Courtesy of Nick Mooney; 31, © Patsy A. Jacks/Shutterstock.

Publisher: Kenn Goin
Senior Editor: Lisa Wiseman
Creative Director: Spencer Brinker
Original Design: Dawn Beard Creative
Photo Researcher: Jennifer Bright

Library of Congress Cataloging-in-Publication Data

Markovics, Joyce L.
  Tasmanian devil : nighttime scavenger / by Joyce L. Markovics.
     p. cm. — (Uncommon animals)
  Includes bibliographical references and index.
  ISBN-13: 978-1-59716-733-8 (library binding)
  ISBN-10: 1-59716-733-9 (library binding)
  1. Tasmanian devil—Juvenile literature. I. Title.

  QL737.M33M37 2009
  599.2'7—dc22
                              2008009307

For more information, write to Bearport Publishing Company, Inc., 101 Fifth Avenue, Suite 6R, New York, New York 10003. Printed in the United States of America.

10 9 8 7 6 5 4 3

Contents

Screams in the Dark

In September 1803, a ship arrived on the island of Tasmania (taz-MAY-nee-*uh*). Captain John Bowen and a group of British **settlers** had come to start a new **community**. Soon after landing, they set up camp.

Tasmanian Aborigines (*ab*-uh-RIJ-uh-neez) were the first people to live in Tasmania. They are shown here along the banks of the Derwent River, the same river that Captain John Bowen and the settlers camped on.

That night, tired from the long trip, the settlers quickly fell asleep. Soon, however, they were awakened by awful screams coming from the dark forest. Gripped by fear, the settlers sat frozen in their tents. What could be making these terrible sounds?

A typical Tasmanian forest filled with eucalyptus (*yoo*-kuh-LIP-tuhss) trees

Tasmania was named after Abel Tasman, a Dutch explorer. He was the first European to discover the land in 1642.

Feared and Hated

When the settlers heard the spine-chilling screams, they pictured an awful beast. The creature sounded so terrible and evil that they named it the Tasmanian devil. Was the mysterious animal as truly terrifying as it sounded? According to George Harris it was.

A recent story tells of Tasmanian devils gobbling up a hiker who had died in a forest. As the story goes, when the hiker was found, only his leg bones and the bottoms of his boots were left.

George Harris was a **surveyor** with an interest in wildlife. In 1806, he became the first European to study Tasmanian devils. Harris used raw meat as **bait** to catch a male and a female devil. He kept them in a large wooden barrel. For two months, he studied the creatures. In his journal, he described them as cruel and "**savage**." He also wrote that their jaws could "crack the largest bones with ease."

George Harris sketched this fierce-looking Tasmanian devil.

Killing the Devils

The stories told by Harris and the other settlers only made people more afraid of the devils. In the 1800s, for example, workers at a wool company were scared that the devils would attack their sheep. They paid hunters to kill the creatures—35 cents for females and 25 cents for males.

Sheep grazing in Tasmania

Farmers in Tasmania also feared the devils. They thought the creatures would kill their **livestock**. So they used poison and traps to get rid of them.

Finally in 1941, to protect the devils from dying out, laws against hunting them were passed. However, tens of thousands of devils had already been killed. Even with the laws, people sometimes still hunt these creatures today.

This devil was caught in an old-fashioned trap.

One farmer killed up to 1,000 devils in a ten-year period.

The Truth About Devils

People in Tasmania had the wrong idea, however. Devils don't usually kill animals for food. They feed mostly on animals that are already dead. Today, scientists know that Tasmanian devils are not the monsters people once thought they were.

The tail of a Tasmanian devil stores fat. A thick tail is a sign of a well-fed devil.

Biologist Nick Mooney has worked with devils for many years. He knows that they're actually shy, small animals— only as big as a medium-sized dog. Generally, devils are so shy that they may even shake when around people. They are not dangerous to humans and they will only attack livestock if the animals are sick or unable to move.

Nick Mooney was born in Tasmania. As a child, he became interested in studying devils and other wildlife.

Uncommon Creatures

Scientists also know that these shy animals are found only in Tasmania, a small group of islands located several hundred miles south of **mainland** Australia. The devils used to live in Australia, too. However, they've been **extinct** there for about 600 years.

Tasmanian Devils in the Wild

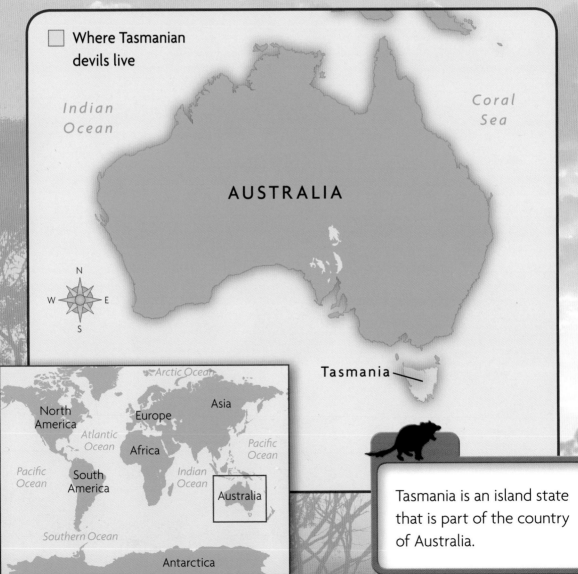

☐ Where Tasmanian devils live

Indian Ocean

Coral Sea

AUSTRALIA

N
W　E
S

Tasmania

Arctic Ocean

North America

Europe

Asia

Atlantic Ocean

Africa

Pacific Ocean

Pacific Ocean

South America

Indian Ocean

Australia

Southern Ocean

Antarctica

Tasmania is an island state that is part of the country of Australia.

Tasmanian devils, like kangaroos and koalas, are **marsupials**. This means that females carry their young in pouches on their bellies. The babies grow inside the pouches until they're too big to fit.

koala

A female devil (center) with her babies, that have grown too big to fit inside her pouch

kangaroo

Night Dwellers

Early on in his research, Nick Mooney learned that these unique creatures wouldn't be easy to study. The reason is that in many areas they come out only at night. During the day, they sleep in **dens**. These homes are under logs or in small caves. Sometimes, though, they make their dens under people's houses, where they're not usually welcome. When this happens, Nick often helps the noisy devils find new homes. Sometimes he is able to convince the homeowners to let the creatures stay.

A devil leaves its den.

At night, the devils' black fur blends into the darkness, making them almost invisible. This gives the young devils protection from large owls and other animals that want to eat them.

Nick and other scientists also discovered that the devils travel far at night to look for food. They use their sharp eyesight, **keen** sense of smell, and good hearing to search for something to eat.

While they live alone, Tasmanian devils will sometimes gather with others to feed. Devils often argue and fight with one another over each bloody bite.

Sometimes devils can be found resting in the sun.

What's for Dinner?

The Tasmanian devil has a huge appetite. It can weigh 15 to 27 pounds (7 to 12 kg) and eat one-third of its body weight in one meal. The devil is both a **predator** and a **scavenger**. It prefers hunting small animals, such as **wombats**, **wallabies**, birds, and insects. However, it feeds mostly on **carrion**, which is easier to find because of its rotten smell.

Tasmanian devils sometimes feed in groups. Tearing apart food with other devils makes it easier to eat

The powerful jaws of the devil are built for tearing large pieces of flesh and for crushing small bones. The devil's jaws are so strong that they can tear apart a wire cage! According to Nick, devils often use their strength to try to escape from the traps he sets for them.

Scientists say that for its size, a devil's jaws are more powerful than a tiger's.

Tasmanian devils have been called "nature's cleanup crew." They eat dead animals that often carry diseases. By getting rid of these animals, the devils decrease the danger of other animals getting sick from them.

Devils in the Home

During his research, Nick has had a very close relationship with these uncommon creatures. He has even had them live in his home. To learn more about them, Nick and his wife, Kate, raised several baby devils that had been **orphaned**. The little animals ran, climbed, and played all over his house. On cold nights, some of the babies would sit in front of the fireplace. They even waited for Nick to light it so that they could warm up!

The devil babies that Nick and Kate raised were very playful with each other. They were also very noisy at night.

Each baby had its own personality. Eric was one of their favorite devils. He had a very quick **temper** and also scared easily. The sight and sound of the vacuum cleaner would send him running to hide in the corner.

Kate quietly checked the orphaned devils—Einy, Meany, Miney, and Moe. At eight months old, they could bite. Kate had to be very careful.

While examining devil droppings in the wild, Nick discovered that the animals ate some unusual things—a sock, the head of a tiger snake, aluminum foil, half a pencil, an owl's foot, and the knee from a pair of jeans.

19

A Screaming Match

Nick's close relationship with the devils helped him learn how they "talk" to one another. They might bark, growl, sneeze, or scream. The animals also hiss and snort to claim a spot on a **carcass**. However, their loud threats over food usually don't end in serious fights.

Nick says that the noises the devils make can sound like a wailing scream or a soft bark.

Male and female devils also scream and snarl at each other during the **mating season**. The male may not allow the female to leave his side for days. Sometimes, he will bite and drag her around by the neck. After they have mated, the fed-up female chases the male away.

This male (right) is biting a female devil. Luckily, they live apart for most of the year.

When devils are angry, their pink ears turn bright red or purple.

In the Pouch

A few weeks after mating, the female devil gives birth to as many as 30 tiny babies, though only a few will survive. Each one is no larger than a grain of rice. After they're born, the newborns climb into their mother's pouch. There they will sleep and feed on milk.

Three-month-old baby devils holding onto their mother

The pouch of a female Tasmanian devil is located near her tail. The young stay inside the pouch until they're about four months old. Then they live in a den where they're cared for by their mother. At nine months old, they're ready to live on their own.

Baby marsupials are usually called joeys. Some people call baby devils imps.

A Devastating Disease

Young and old, all Tasmanian devils have to deal with a new danger. Many of these animals have died from Devil Facial Tumor Disease (DFTD). This is a type of cancer that causes huge growths on the devils' faces.

This devil has DFTD. The tumors grow so large that they can push out teeth and prevent the animals from eating. In time, the devils starve to death.

Scientists first saw devils with this disease in 1996. At that time, the **population** of devils on Tasmania was about 150,000. In 2006, it was down to between 20,000 and 50,000. Scientists are still not sure what causes the disease but they think they know how it spreads. "We suspect it mainly spreads by biting when animals quarrel or mate," Nick explains. So far, every devil that has been found with the disease has been killed by it within six months.

DFTD is the leading cause of adult devil deaths. Car accidents, dog attacks, and **habitat** destruction are responsible for some, too.

Nick Mooney invented a special trap to safely capture and study sick devils.

What's to Come?

Today, many zoos have joined DFTD treatment and **breeding** programs in hope of saving the **species**. Scientists are also studying the disease in **laboratories** to find the cause and a cure.

This devil is undergoing a checkup to see if he has DFTD.

Due to DFTD, devils face a high risk of dying out. In 2008, the Tasmanian government listed the devil as an **endangered** species.

According to Nick, without more work the devils might disappear forever. He says that if the animals in zoos also get the disease, "devils may be headed for extinction." Nick and the other scientists hope their work will allow the Tasmanian devil to continue screaming its eerie song.

Today, people in Tasmania are proud of the devil. The animals are a popular symbol of the state.

Tasmanian Devil Facts

The Tasmanian devil is a marsupial. Like all marsupials, it gives birth to young that are very small. After they're born, the young climb into the mother's pouch where they feed on milk for about four months. At about ten months of age, they are ready to live on their own. Here are some other facts about this uncommon animal.

Weight	**adult males:** usually about 19 pounds (9 kg) **adult females:** usually about 15 pounds (7 kg)
Height	**adult males:** 12 inches (30 cm) tall **adult females:** 10 inches (25 cm) tall
Fur Color	black, with white stripes on the chest or backside
Food	dead animals mostly, but will also hunt wombats, wallabies, birds, tadpoles, moths, and other small animals
Life Span	6 years in the wild, 8 years in zoos
Habitat	Tasmania
Population	anywhere from 20,000 to 50,000 in the wild

More Uncommon Animals

The Tasmanian devil is one kind of uncommon animal found in Tasmania. Many other types of unusual animals also live there.

Eastern Quoll

- The eastern quoll (KWOL) is called the "native cat."
- It's a marsupial about the size of a house cat and lives only in Tasmania.
- Like the Tasmanian devil, it eats meat and insects, and is active mostly at night.
- The quoll's spotted fur helps it blend into its forest or grassland environment.
- Quolls give birth to up to 30 young, but the mother can only care for 6.

Tasmanian Pademelon

- Tasmanian pademelons (PAD-ee-*mel*-uhnz) are marsupials that look like small kangaroos with pointy noses and short tails.
- The creatures thump the ground with their feet to warn other pademelons of danger.
- They feed at night, eating young plants, leaves, and short green grass.
- In the wild, they may live up to six years.

Glossary

bait (BAYT) food used to attract an animal to a trap

biologist (bye-OL-uh-jist) a scientist who studies plants or animals

breeding (BREED-ing) producing young

carcass (KAR-kuhss) the dead body of an animal

carrion (KA-ree-uhn) rotting meat

community (kuh-MYOO-nuh-tee) a group of people who live in the same area

dens (DENZ) a hidden place where an animal sleeps or has its babies

endangered (en-DAYN-jurd) in danger of dying out

extinct (ek-STINGKT) when a kind of plant or animal has died out

habitat (HAB-uh-*tat*) a place in nature where a plant or animal normally lives

keen (KEEN) very sharp

laboratories (LAB-ruh-*tor*-eez) places where scientific experiments are carried out

livestock (LIVE-*stok*) animals, such as sheep, that are raised by people on farms or ranches

mainland (MAYN-luhnd) the largest land mass of a country

marsupials (mar-SOO-pee-uhlz) a group of animals in which the young are raised in pouches found on the mothers' bellies

mating season (MAYT-ing SEE-zuhn) the time of year when animals breed

orphaned (OR-fuhnd) left without parents

population (*pop*-yuh-LAY-shuhn) the total number of a kind of animal living in a place

predator (PRED-uh-tur) an animal that hunts other animals for food

savage (SAV-ij) not tame; dangerous

scavenger (SKAV-uhn-jur) an animal that feeds on dead animals

settlers (SET-lurz) people who make their home in a new place

species (SPEE-sheez) groups that animals are divided into according to similar characteristics; members of the same species can have offspring together

surveyor (sur-VAY-ur) a person who inspects things, such as land, for quality

temper (TEM-pur) a tendency to get angry

wallabies (WOL-uh-*beez*) small marsupials that are part of the kangaroo family

wombats (WOM-bats) Australian animals that look like small bears

Bibliography

Blakeslee, Sandra. "In Tasmania, the Devil Now Faces Its Own Hell." *The New York Times* (May 31, 2005).

Flanagan, Richard. "Tasmania." *The New York Times* (September 12, 2004).

Owen, David, and David Pemberton. *Tasmanian Devil: A Unique and Threatened Animal.* Crows Nest, Australia: Allen & Unwin (2005).

Read More

Collard III, Sneed B. *Pocket Babies and Other Amazing Marsupials.* Plain City, OH: Darby Creek Publishing (2007).

Darling, Kathy. *Tasmanian Devil: On Location.* New York: HarperCollins (1992).

Markle, Sandra. *Tasmanian Devils (Animal Scavengers).* Minneapolis, MN: Lerner Publications Company (2006).

Steele, Christy. *Tasmanian Devil (Animals of the Rain Forest).* Chicago: Raintree (2003).

Learn More Online

To learn more about Tasmanian devils, visit
www.bearportpublishing.com/UncommonAnimals

Index

About the Author

Joyce L. Markovics is an editor, writer, and orchid collector.
She has a great affection for marsupials and other unusual animals.
She lives with her husband, Adam, and their pet aquatic frog.